How to Boost 100 Points in 30 Days Even With Zero Credit History

Robbie Seng

Copyright © 2020 Robbie Seng Version 2

All rights reserved. No part of this publication may be reproduced, stored in, or introduced into a retrieval system, or transmitted, in any form, or by any means (electronic, mechanical, photocopying, recording, or otherwise) without the prior written permission of the copyright owner of this book and is illegal and punishable by law.

Although the author and publisher have made every effort to ensure that the information in this book was correct at press time, the author and publisher do not assume and hereby disclaim any liability to any party for any loss, damage, or disruption caused by errors or omissions, whether such errors or omissions result from negligence, accident, or any other cause.

This book is for entertainment purposes only. The views expressed are those of the author alone and should not be taken as expert instruction or commands. The reader is responsible for his or her own actions.
Neither the author nor the publisher assumes any responsibility or liability whatsoever on the behalf of the purchaser or reader of these materials. Any perceived slight of any individual or organization is purely unintentional.

Table of Contents

Introduction   5

Zero Credit History- What is means?   5

I Have No Credit History   6

What is a Credit Score?   7

What a Good Score is   8

How your Score is Calculated   9

More than one Score   11

Why You need a Good Score   12

What is not Included in My Credit Score   13

Advantage of Credit Score   13

A Credit Score is Different from a Credit Report   15

Starting Point for your Score   16

Have Zero Credit- Tips to Boost Score   17

Boosted Score from Zero Credit- Now What?   23

Tips to Boost Your Score Further   25

Tips May Work Different Users   29

Financial Mistakes to Avoid   30

Taking Advantage of a Good Score   32

Final Words   33

References   34

Download Your Free Gift Now

Discover Simple Hacks to

Nourish & Nurture Your Brain for Top Performance

Without Any Complications.

As a way of saying "thank you" for your purchase, I'm going to share with you a

Free Gift that is exclusive to readers of "**How to Boost Your Credit Score by 100 points**".

Even with ZERO Credit History

Follow link below to check it out

https://rchongseng.clickfunnels.com/optin1605558798839

Introduction

You might not be aware, but your credit score is one of the most important measures of your credit health. In fact, it could prove to be a deciding factor when taking a loan from a bank or any other financial institution. This is because it gives lenders a quick idea of your creditworthiness.

So, every time you set any major financial goal, such as buying a home or a car, your credit score is highly likely to come into the picture. It would help lenders decide whether you qualify for a loan, and if yes, then at what terms. So, the higher the score is, the better it is.

Thinks of credit score like a report card that gives an overview of a students' performance at the end of a term. Unlike the grades in the report card, your financial activity is in a scoring range.

Thus, it is important that you always strive to increase your score. If somehow, your score is not up to the mark, you should not worry because you can easily boost it with the help of a few simple tricks.

Even for those with zero credit history, having a good credit score is especially important. This is because you might not need credit now, but you never know what the future holds for you. So, it is best that you start working on building your credit score from now on to ensure you do not face issues when you need it the most.

Zero Credit History – What it Means?

If you have not used credit ever, or in a long time, it is possible that you have no credit score. This is certainly not a great situation to be in, but the good news is that you can fix it easily.

Having a no credit score is not the same as having a bad score. One has a bad score because of a bad financial history, such as due to bankruptcy, missing EMIs, defaulting on loans and more. On the other hand, no credit means you have not had any recent credit activity that the credit bureaus can use to come up with a score for you.

There may be a few reasons why you may not have a score, including you are young and have just started earning. Or, you have not used any credit recently. Even if you have used credit recently, it is possible that you have no score. This could happen if the lender does not report your credit to the credit bureaus or report it to only one bureau. It is not mandatory for the lenders to share your credit activities with the credit bureaus, but most do as it eventually helps them to evaluate the borrowers.

Another reason why you may have a zero-credit history is you have relocated to a new country. Irrespective of your old credit history, some countries require to re-build your credit history if you have relocated.

I Have No Credit History - Do I Need to Worry?

No, not at all, there is nothing to worry. You can easily and quickly build your score from zero. Moreover, you do not need the help of any expert, or hire someone to do it for you. You yourself can do it from the comfort of your home and that too, without investing too much time. All you must do is follow the tips detailed later, and you will see your score accelerate from zero to a reasonable one in no time.

However, before we detail those steps, it is important for you to understand what a credit score is and how it works.

What is a Credit Score?

A credit score is a three-digit number that speaks a great deal about your financial standing. The more this number, the better a borrower looks to the potential lenders. Basically, the lender uses it to determine whether to give you a loan, and if yes, then how much.

Also, a higher score would mean lenders offering more affordable terms, such as a lower interest rate. We can also say that lenders use it to determine the probability a person would be able to pay the loan in a timely manner. Your credit score is based on several factors, including past debts, repayment history, number of accounts and more (discussed later).

Fair Isaac Corporation, popularly known as FICO, created the credit score model that is now used by most financial institutions. Though other credit-scoring systems are also there, the FICO score is the most popular and widely used.

A FICO score ranges from 350 to 850, where the former means extremely high risk and the latter extremely low risk. In the U.S., the average FICO score hit bottom in 2009, at 689, while in 2018, it made a new high of 704.

Another popular scoring model is Vantage Score. It was developed in 2006 and had a slightly different approach than FICO. A lender, in this method, considers average available credit, credit utilization, recent credit, credit balances, payment history, and depth of credit. This method gives the biggest weight to payment history and credit utilization.

A Vantage Score range between 300 to 850. It must be noted that the first two versions of the Vantage Score ranged from 501 to 990. The Vantage Score range was changed to make it easier for users to compare their Vantage Score and FICO scores.

Though Vantage Score is gaining acceptance, it is not as popular as FICO. Also, unlike FICO, Vantage Score does not calculate industry-specific scores.

What a Good Score is?

There are as such no hard and fast rules defining a good credit score. Different lenders have different criteria on how to use the credit score, and they evaluate the credit score on a case-by-case basis.

Generally, people with a score of less than 640 are subprime borrowers. Lenders charge higher interest on the subprime mortgages than the conventional mortgage. The higher interest rate compensates the lender for taking a higher risk in giving a loan to a subprime borrower. Along with higher interest rate, such borrowers may get a shorter repayment term or are required to get a co-signer as well.

Talking about a good credit score, generally, a score of 700 and more is seen as good. A borrower with such a score may get favorable payment terms, such as a lower interest rate. If a borrower has a score of 800 and above, it is seen asexcellent.Though every creditor has its own criteria for the credit score, the average FICO score range that many lenders use is:

SCORE	REMARK
300 to 579	Poor
580 to 669	Fair
670 to 739	Good
740 to 799	Very Good
800 to 850	Excellent

How Your Score Is Calculated?

If you know and understand how your score is calculated, then you yourself can figure out ways to boost your credit score. Primarily, there are five factors that credit bureaus use to calculate your credit score. Different agencies may give different weight to these factors, but these are the five factors that financial agencies use to calculate your score. These five factors are:

1. **Payment history**

This is certainly the most important component for calculating your credit score. In the FICO score, it carries a 35% weight.

The payment history that impacts your score includes, student loans, mortgage loans, auto loans, credit cards, instalment loans, finance company accounts, home equity loans, as well as retail department store accounts.

Your payment history reveals a lot about yourself, such as whether you make timely payments, when did you miss the payment, how many days after the due date you made the payment, any recent payment you missed, and much more.

The credit history will also reveal the number of your credit accounts that are delinquent in comparison to all your accounts. Further, the credit history will also include the details of bankruptcies, foreclosures, and wage attachments.

The better your payment history is, the higher your score will be. It must be noted that a single missed payment can have a negative impact on your score.

2. Amount owed

This is the next important factor, and it carries a 30% weight in the FICO score. If you have many credit accounts and owing money on them does not necessarily make a high-risk borrower and reduces your score. Rather, if you have used most or all your available credit, it may suggest a risky proposition. For the lenders, it could mean that you have more chances of defaulting.

An ideal credit utilization ratio, which is the percentage of available credit to used, is less than 30%. Though this component basically focuses on the current debt, it does consider the number of different type of accounts a lender has. For instance, if you have a massive amount of debt from several sources, this could lower your credit score. Similarly, high balance and maxed-out credit cards would push your score down.

3. Length of credit history

The duration of your credit history, or how long your debt lasts, also play a crucial role in determining your credit score. In the FICO score, this component holds a 15% weight. This means that individuals who have not been using credit for long may have a higher credit score.

The length of credit history basically includes, the age of your newest and oldest credit accounts, as well as the average age of all your accounts. Also, it may look at the age of the specific credit accounts and how long have you used specific accounts. In all, we can say that with the length of credit history, a lender tries to gauze whether a borrower has a history of responsibly paying off the credit accounts.

4. Credit mix

Credit bureaus consider the mix of your loans and debts as well. These include instalment loans, credit cards, mortgage loans, retail accounts and finance company accounts. The more mix of credit accounts, the better your score is. It is not necessary to have one of each, but having a mix is better from the point of view of the score. In the FICO score, it carries a 10% weight.

5. New credit

This also carries a 10% weight in the FICO score. Generally, opening many credit accounts in a short period of time is seen as a risk. This is true, especially for those having a long credit history. So, it is better to avoid opening too many accounts quickly.

More Than One Score – Yes, It is Possible

You will be surprised to know that you could have more than one score at the same time. This could be because of many reasons, such as scores from different companies, a different method of calculating the data, or the difference in data for calculating the score.

In the U.S., there are three major credit bureaus – TransUnion, Equifax, and Experian. It is very much possible that the score of the same individual from different credit bureaus could be different. This could be because the same information or data might not be available to all the bureaus. Additionally, the financial models used by these bureaus could also give different results, even if they use the same data.

Another reason for more than one score is because lenders and creditors may use different scores depending on their industry. For instance, if you are planning to buy a car and approach an auto lender, then this lender might use a score that focuses more on your credit history in relation to auto loans. It is also possible that lenders use all scores combined to come up with a blended credit score.

Why Do You Need a Good Score (or Even a Score)?

Having a good score or even a score will give you enormous benefits both in terms of convenience and financial perspective.

One of the first benefits is access to good credit cards. A credit card is a must for shopping, be it a retail store, restaurant, gas station and mall. It allows you to shop online as well, and even public transit systems use automated machines that accept payment through a credit card.

Along with credit cards, a credit score is important when you plan to make bigger purchases also. For instance, if you wish to purchase a car and seek a loan, then the lender and the dealership will look at your credit score, among other things.

Moreover, if you want to rent an apartment, then a credit check is part of the vetting process. Even cable companies and utilities review your credit score, and if it is not good, then you may be asked to give a higher security deposit.

Often prospective employers look at your credit rating before deciding on whether to offer you a job.

These are just a few instances when a credit score comes handy. In real life, a good credit score will continue to help you in almost every phase of your life. It will not be wrong to say that it could prove your best friend for life provided you do not leave it as well.

What's Not Included in My Credit Score?

Your credit score basically includes all your financial details of past and present. There are, however, a few of your details that a credit score does not include. Such as:

- Nationality, race, religion, marital status, sex, and color.
- Age and address.
- Details about your salary, employer, employment history, and designation. Lenders, however, may use this information in making a final decision.
- Your score also does not include soft inquiries. These are the inquiries that are usually initiated by others, such as companies making promotional credit offers. Also, when you check your own credit report, or use credit monitoring services, they come under soft inquiries. Such inquiries do not impact the credit score.

Advantage of Credit Score

Whenever you approach any lender for a debt or credit, your credit score is likely the first thing that they check on you. The same is true for any type of debt you may go for, be it a card, a loan, or a mortgage. A credit score easily gives a lender a glimpse of your financial standing and creditworthiness. In a way, it helps the lender with the risk assessment of the borrower.

More importantly, a good credit score could prove immensely useful to you over your lifetime and that too in varying ways. Following are the advantages or benefits of having a good credit score:

1. Low interest rates and better credit terms

This is the most obvious benefit of having a good credit score. Those having a good score, get loans, credit card and other debt at a lower interest rate. Along with a lower interest rate, a good score may also get you entitled to a discount or waiver on the processing fee. Also, such a borrower gets eligible for a higher loan amount.

2. Improve chances for credit card and loan approval

Those with a good credit score are less risky. Thus, they have more chances of being approved for a loan and credit cards. Moreover, you stand a higher chance of getting a credit card that offers better rewards and benefits, such as cashback, travel points, and more.

3. Higher credit card limits

In addition to a lower interest rate on credit cards and loan, a good score will automatically make you eligible for a higher limit on the credit card. On the other hand, a bad score may reduce your credit limit. A good score speaks well about your financial reputations; thus, lenders feel safe offering you a higher limit.

4. Eligible for pre-approved loan

Having a good credit score may also make you eligible for pre-approved loan. Banks often offer the pre-approved loan to their existing clients who have a good credit history. Along with the pre-approved loan, a good score also helps you to quickly get approval for the loans.

5. Good for visa application

Along with providing financial benefits, a good score also adds weightage to your visa application. Many countries, including the U.S. and U.K., consider tax records of the individuals who apply for a visa. Thus, if you have a good credit score, it increases your visa approval chances.

6. Future benefits

If you do not have debt or loan and feel that you need not worry about the credit score, then you are wrong. You may not have a debt now, or currently do not have any plan to take debt in a near period, but the future is certain. You may never know when things go wrong, and you may have to resort to debt to stabilize your financial condition. Thus, it is especially important that you maintain your credit score so that in future when you need, it is there to back you.

A Credit Score is Different from a Credit Report

So far, we have been talking about credit score and credit report. I have seen people confusing the two and using both interchangeably. So, before we move to the main part, I feel it is important to clear out the differences between the two.

A credit report gives a more holistic view of your financial health, detailing information about present credit situation and financial activities. It also carries your personal information, detail of credit accounts, public records, as well as inquiries into your credit.

Your credit score, on the other hand, is a proxy for the health of your credit reports. Or, we can say, if you or the lender does not have time to review your credit report, then the credit score could give a glimpse into your financial standing.

Starting Point for Your Score

Now you know all about credit score and are ready for the tried and tested tips that will help you to boost your score by 100 points in 30 days even if you have no credit history. Before we detail those tips, there is one more thing that you need to know that will help you with your score.

If you have zero credit history and a zero score, and you are starting to build your score with new credit, it does not mean that you will start at 300 (the base score). A score of 300 is exceedingly rare, even for those making devastating financial mistakes. So, it is very unlikely for a person with no credit history to start at a score of 300.

Think of it like a quiz in a class which you are not able to attend because you have an appointment with the dentist. Not able to attend is quite different from being present in the class and answering all questions incorrectly.

Answering questions incorrectly is like making financial mistakes that result in lowering your score. Not attending the class is same as no data for credit bureaus to evaluate you. The teacher would eventually evaluate you with the next quiz.

Similarly, if credit bureaus have no information on you, they cannot evaluate you. But once you start using credit, they would have some data to calculate your score. Your score will certainly be in top range, but it would not be at the bottom either.

One Important Point

Before you go these tips, it is recommended that you request a free credit report from the credit reporting agencies. In the U.S., you are entitled to get one free report from each of the three agencies each year.

If you do not have any credit history, but there is still a file on you, it should ring a warning bell. It is possible that the agency has mixed someone else's credit detail against your name, or someone else might be using your identity to get the credit. If such is the case, then before you start to build up your score, you must get such disputes cleared.

You need to contact the agency, show them the proof, and get your name cleared.

Have ZERO Credit - Tips to Boost Score

Now you are ready for the tips that will help you to boost your credit score very quickly. These tips are tried and tested both in real-life and experiments, and their success rate 100% provided you implement them accurately. Remember all these tricks are easy, and you do not need an outsider to do it for you. You can do it yourself.

1. Become an authorized user

This is the easiest way to boost your credit. All you must do is become an authorized user on a credit card of a family member or friend. This will help you to create your own credit history without getting your credit card. This way, you also have zero liability and it's risk-free as well.

However, before becoming an authorized user, you need to ensure that the family member or friend has good credit and he or she uses the credit card sensibly. You should avoid becoming an authorized user on an account that does not have a good credit history. Such negative actions of the primary cardholder would reflect on your credit history and may ruin your score.

The thing you need to be careful about is practicing responsible behavior with the card. You should have a clear plan on how you will repay the purchases you make with the card so that the primary cardholder does not feel the burden.

2. Apply for secured credit card

Credit cards are one of the best ways to build your score. Along with becoming an authorized user, you can also go for a secured credit card to build your score. A secured card is relatively easier to get even if one has a poor or no credit history at all. You may get such a card with a security deposit of just $500.

It works just like any other credit card and helps you to establish a credit history provided you manage it responsibly. A secured card, like a traditional card, also has a limit, incurs interest charges, and may even offer you reward.

The only major difference between a secured and regular card is that in the former you need to make a security deposit to get the line of credit. Generally, the amount you make as security deposit becomes your credit limit.

There are many secured cards available in the market and a simple Google search will help you choose one. For instance, Discover it® Secured card is one of the best secure cards. It offers cashback, a handsome welcome bonus, no annual fee, as well as no additional fees for purchases made outside the U.S. Another good option is Guaranteed Secured Mastercard by Capital One.

Applying and getting such cards is easy as well because there are fewer requirements. Once you get the card, it is important that you use it responsibly. Using responsibly means paying the due amount on time, being on top of the due dates, and ensure that no payments are missed. To make sure you do not miss the due dates, you can set up alerts and reminder to keep track of very payment due.

A secured credit card is different from the prepaid card because the latter does not send credit history to the credit bureaus. Once you have boosted your credit score, you can un-unsubscribe this card, and go for a regular card.

3. **Get a store card**

Nowadays, several retailers and gas stations offer their branded credit card to build loyalty. A customer gets these cards even if they have no credit history, but most do not use it. It is recommended that if you have any such cards then you use it, but do not overspend from it. Also, make sure that you pay the due amount before the due date. Before you start using it, you can ask the retailer or gas station whether they report the credit history to credit bureaus. If they do not, then there is no point in using those cards.

4. Credit-builder loans

The only purpose of these loans is to help users boost their credit score. A user gets this loan only after they have made the payment for it. The lender, in this case, reports the transaction to the credit bureaus. It not just helps you to create a credit history, but also allows you to save a small emergency fund at the end of a loan term. You can get such loans from the credit unions and community banks.

5. Find a co-signer

If you know someone who has a good credit score, and is ready to co-sign a loan for you, then it could easily build your credit score.

You, however, need to repay the loan on or before the due date. It is not easy to find someone ready to co-sign a loan. This is because a co-signor is personally liable for the loan if you are unable to pay the loan. If the co-signor also fails to pay the loan, then it would damage the credit rating for both of you.

6. Report utilities and rent payments to credit bureaus

Paying bills on time is a great way to build the score. Thus, it is crucial that you pay all your bills on time. Also, do confirm with your utility service provider, such as water, electric, gas and more, whether they report the payments to the credit bureaus.

7. Take a student credit card

You can also go for a student credit card to build your score. These cards are designed for young borrowers, and thus, come with a few limitations, such as low borrowing limits. Also, these cards generally have higher interest rates. Thus, it is important that you do not apply for such a card if you are not confident of paying it back.

8. Go easy on the number of cards

Having a secured or a student credit card is obviously a good way to boost your score. But you should not just start accumulating cards. If you apply for two or more cards around the same time, it may send a wrong signal to the credit bureaus. It is recommended that there is a gap of a few months between the two cards you apply for.

9. Beware of identity theft

This trick would not help you to boost your score but would ensure that your score does not go down because of identity theft. To check for identity theft, you should regularly verify your monthly bills to make sure all the purchases on it are by you only. There have been cases when hackers stole financial credentials and made purchases using it without the user, even realizing. Another way to check is requesting the free credit report from credit bureaus. You can then check the report to ensure all activities belongs to you.

10. Get a secured loan

Like a secured credit card, there is a secured loan. A secured loan is one that is backed by collateral. For instance, if you are taking a loan, then you can put your car as collateral. Such a loan is a good way to boost your score. However, you must pay it back, otherwise, it could damage your score, plus you also lose your asset.

11. Take help of non-profit lending circles

There are organizations, such as the Mission Asset Fund (MAF) that assist low-income borrowers with financing. Such organizations not just provide affordable loans to the borrowers, but also send positive credit history with the credit bureaus.

12. Finance an in-store purchase

You can also make use of store's financing option to create your credit history. Often retailers allow customers to buy expensive items on instalments, or on credit at 0% interest. Such purchases are a type of loan, and thus, paying it on or before the due date helps in establishing a credit history. Before going for such financing option, do read the fine print carefully to ensure there are no hidden fees or unfavorable terms.

13. Booster services

If you are not comfortable with the credit card thing, there is an alternative. Many financial services firms offer tools to build the credit score, but most of them charge a fee for it. Some services firms do offer free tools as well, such as Experian.

Experian Boost allows you to get credit for paying regular bills, such as utility, streaming service, mobile and more. All you must do is pay the bills on time, and your score will automatically get a boost. A point to note is that not all services qualify. For instance, the qualifying streaming payments under Experian Boost are Netflix, Starz, Disney+, HBO and Hulu.

Using these booster services is easy as well. All you need to do is integrate your bank account, which you use to pay utility and other services, verify your credentials and you are ready to go. Once you register, you will get regular updates on your credit score, as well as a detailed credit report.

14. Sign up to have rent payments reported

Along with reporting your monthly bills, you can use a third-party service to report your monthly rent payment to the credit bureaus. Generally, rent payment is not reported to credit bureaus, nor it is used to calculate the credit score. But there are third-party services that report your rent payment details to bureaus. These services, however, charge a fee for this, and your landlord also needs to approve such a thing.

Boosted Score from Zero Credit – Now What?

Now you would have boosted your credit score (from zero credit) using the above tips, but what now?

You should not get complacent that you now have a good score, and it would remain so. Remember, like everything else, your score could also change because you now have a credit history. So, it is important that you make efforts to maintain or even boost your score further.

Again, doing this is no rocket science, and you yourself can do it without spending too much time. In fact, you just need to follow the basics, and it is possible that you might be already practicing such basics.

The very first thing that you need to do to boost your score further is to review your credit report. It will give you an idea about your credit health, including the positive and negative points. Remember that in the U.S. you are entitled to one free report a year, and it is easy to request for a credit report as well.

Reviewing your report also helps to check for errors and get them corrected quickly. As per the FTC (Federal Trade Commission), one in five users has errors in at least one of their credit reports. These errors could range from late payments, fraudulent payments and more, and could negatively impact your score.

A point to note is that a credit bureau has 30 days from the day they get your request, to finish their investigation. If they are unable to verify the accuracy of the dispute, then they delete that item, and this helps to build the score.

There have been instances where people got 5 or more accounts removed within 30 days just by disputing them. Of course, these people have a greater number of accounts, but the idea here is that you should not shy away from disputing from what is not yours.

Reading a credit report is also easy and even laymen can understand it as well. Generally, a credit report carries the following information:

1. Personal information

This section of the report contains your 'vitals' including your name, social security number, birth date, address, current and previous employers, and more. It does not include information on your marital status, education, medical history, political preferences, criminal records, bank account balances and other information not related to credit.

2. Trade account information

This section will carry details on all your open credit accounts. The details will include creditor's name, account number, the amount owed, available credit limit, whether any payment has been made, and time of payment. This section will also include data on the closed accounts, such as payment history for those accounts and whether those accounts were closed in good standing. It will also include information on any missed or late payment and charge-offs.

3. Public record information

A credit report will also have information on you, if any, from the courts, such as bankruptcy filings. Any public record information on you could have a negative effect on your score.

4. Credit inquiries

A credit report also includes hard inquiries, which are based on the actions you have taken, such as applying for credit or financing. There are soft inquiries as well that are the result of the action taken by others. This includes promotional offers of creditor a periodic review of your account by a lender. There can also be soft inquiries when you use credit monitoring services, but these do not impact your score.

Tips to Boost Your Score Further

Now that you have reviewed your report and feel that you need to raise it further, the following tips will help you maintain and boost your score further:

1. Pay bills on time, every time

As you might have realized by now that your payment history matters a lot, no matter how small it is. So, you must make it a habit, if you do not already, to pay all your bills on or before time, be it a utility bill, phone bill, internet bill and more.

2. Do not use all your credit

If you have a credit, it is recommended that you do not use your entire credit limit. Generally, the lower your balance is, the better it is. But having a balance of 30% of your limit is ideal for your score. For example, if your credit limit is $5,000, you must not use more than $1,500 at a time.

3. Go for mix accounts

Now that you have a credit score, it is likely that you may go for more loan or credit. If you have any such plans, it is recommended that you go for a mix of account types, such as instalment loans (like auto loan), and revolving debt (like credit cards).

4. Raise your available credit

Once you have established a credit history, you can boost your score by requesting a higher credit limit from your current creditor. You can easily request to raise your limit. Some lenders allow you to make a request online.

5. Reduce credit utilization

Credit utilization is the ratio of your balance to the credit limit. Ideally, your credit utilization should be less than 30%. So, if your credit utilization is more, then make efforts to bring it down. For instance, you can pay more than your EMI of a loan or make a large payment on your credit card. This could improve your credit utilization.

6. Balance transfer credit card or peer-to-peer loan

If you want to improve your credit utilization, but do not have enough money, then one best way to do it is to go for a balance transfer credit card or peer-to-peer loan. Such credit comes with a much lower interest rate, meaning you could pay off your debt faster. But you should apply for this debt only if you believe that you have a chance at approval. If not, it could impact your score, but if approved, you will be relieved from paying high interest.

7. Do not close your old cards

Even if you have got a new card, then make sure that your old card does not get close due to inactivity. The length of your credit history is one of the most important factors determining your credit score. One thing that lenders want to see is you having positive, long-standing relationships with your existing lenders.

Thus, it is crucial that you maintain your old cards. If you believe using your old card will put you in debt, then use such cards for small purchases only. And pay them off as quickly as possible. This way, you can continue using the old card without incurring too much interest.

8. Cleanup your negative credit history

You may ask the lender or debt collector to share information with the bureaus that may not be entirely true or Pay for delete. Basically, it is a process where you tell the borrower that you will make the payment in full only if the lender promises to delete the negative account history from your credit report.

There are also late payment adjustments, or the goodwill letters. Borrowers wrote these letters to lenders urging them not to include the late payment information in their credit report.

One late payment has the potential to drop your credit score by 60 to 110 points. How much your score drops depend on your current score as well. For instance, I have seen people with a score of 680 saw their score drop by 60 to 80 points because of a 30-day late payment. For the same score, a 90-day late payment could lead to a drop of 70 to 90 points.

Similarly, a 30-day late payment for a 780 score may drop your score by 90 to 110 points, while a 90-day late payment can lower your score by 105 to 135 points.

However, actions such as Pay for delete and goodwill letters are not ethical, and thus might violate the Fair Credit Reporting Act (FCRA). This act requires the lender to do fair and accurate credit reporting.

"Unfair credit reporting methods undermine the public confidence, which is essential to the continued functioning of the banking system," FCRA says.

9. Know when creditor reports payment history

Knowing when your card issuer reports your payment history to the credit bureaus could also help. Just call or email your card issuer for this. Usually, it is the closing date or the last day of the billing cycle of your account. This date, however, is different from your "due date."

Always try to make the payment not before the due date, but before the reporting date. Because if you make the payment after the reporting date, then your reported balance to the bureaus could be high (even if you pay before the due date), and this negatively impacts your ratio. So, it is recommended that you pay before the closing date, this way your reported balance will be low.

10. Watch out for Joint Applicants

Just like you ask someone with a good score to be a co-signor to a loan, anyone else may also ask you to be a co-signor for their loan. Now, if that other person defaults on their loan, then it would negatively affect your score and reflect in your report as well. The best way to prevent it is not to be a co-signor at all, and if you become a co-signor, then make sure the other person is of good credit health and always make payment on-time.

Tips May Work Differently for Different Users

As said before, there are different scoring models, and they have a different approach to calculate your score. Also, everyone's score does not get affected the same way despite taking the same exact actions. For instance, if you and your friend have the same score and follow the above tips as it is, then also it is possible that your scores may differ. This might sound confusing, but it's true. Let us look at some examples to get a better understanding:

- Suppose Mr. A has a history of making all payments on-time, but he forgets to pay one bill in the last month. Mr. B also forgets to pay one bill in the last month, but he has a track record of making late payments. The score of Mr. A will not get affected the same way as Mr. B. In fact, Mr. A may even call up his card issuer and explain the reason why he failed to pay on-time and request them not to report this to the credit bureaus. The issuer will not entertain the same request from Mr. B because of his payment history.

- As said above hard credit inquiries may also negatively affect your score by about 4-10 points per inquiry. Suppose Mr. C fills out an application, but it's his fourth application in 30 days. Mr. D also fills out an application, but he only filled one application in last 30 days. It is more likely that Mr. C's score will drop more than Mr. D.

Suppose Mr. E and F raised their credit limit by $800 (total limit now $1,300). Mr. E's balance was zero previously, so with new limit he has $1,300 in open credit. Mr. F's

- balance, on the other hand, was $500 before, so he now has $800 in credit. This means, both performed the same action, but the outcome is different.

Financial Mistakes to Avoid

So now you have created your credit history and know how to maintain and boost it. But you are not done yet. There is still something you need to know that would help you with your financial score, and it is the common financial mistakes that most people make. Such mistakes can undermine your efforts to build your credit, and thus, it is important that you avoid them and make it a habit to stay away from them forever. Following are the common mistakes that you need to avoid:

1. **Spending more than what you can afford**

It is common sense that spending more than one's income can put them in debt. But many people continue to accumulate debt for varying reasons, including maintaining their lavish lifestyle. A simple way to know your spending limit is to calculate your debt-to-income ratio. An ideal ratio as per the financial experts is between 40 to 50%. To calculate this ratio, you need to divide all your monthly debt obligations by gross monthly income. A person with a ratio on the higher side is more likely to face issue in meeting monthly payments.

2. **No budget**

If you have a budget, it keeps a check on your spending and helps you with money management as well. With a budget, you have an idea of how much you are spending and how much is your saving. Without a budget, you just keep spending with no proper record of your financial transactions. You can always review your budget to cut on the items that you are overspending, or you do not need.

3. Not comparing instalment loans

If you are planning to go for an instalment loan, such as auto or mortgage, then you should treat it like any other buying decision. This means, you should shop for these loans, i.e., compare plans of different financial institutions and then select the best possible deal. When you shop for a loan, you can get the lowest available interest rates, as well as fees and service charges.

4. Failing to take fraud preventive measures

There are several laws and regulations to protect users from credit fraud. Even lenders, such as credit card companies and banks take measures, to protect them and their clients from fraud. However, all these measures may prove ineffective if you are being careless. Thus, it is particularly important that you take measures to protect yourself.

One such measure is reviewing your monthly credit card statements and credit report. Another small but useful step is not keeping cards in your wallet that you do not need. You must also destroy the statements and receipts that carry your account number. Moreover, you should also be careful when clicking on links sent from anonymous source. These measures will not directly help you to boost your score but will assist you in ensuring that your score does not deteriorate with no fault of yours.

5. Applying for too much credit in a small amount of time

Taking on too much debt in a short time sends a wrong signal and could indicate to a lender that you may take more credit than what you could repay. Moreover, it also increases the number of hard inquiries you make and negatively affects your balance-to-limit ratio.

Taking Advantage of a Good Score

Now that you have boosted your credit score, you will get the usual benefits that come along with it, such as lower interest rate, quick approval and more. Along with these usual benefits, you can also use your new (improved) score to get better terms of your existing debt and obligations.

With improved (good) score, banks and other lenders consider you a good risk and you become a valued customer to them.

Thus, they would never want to lose you and would compete hard to make sure rivals do not poach you. So, you can take benefit of this by renegotiating terms with your existing lenders

For instance, you can renegotiate your auto insurance if your credit score has improved substantially since you first took the policy. Generally, the insurer will not check your score at the time of renewing. So, you will have to ask the insurer to recalculate the premium after applying the new score. In case you are not satisfied, you can look for other insurers as well. You can do the same with other debts as well.

This way, you can save a reasonable amount of money. You can either invest the savings that you generate from such negotiations, or you can use those savings to further improve your score by paying off debts.

Final Words

Your credit score is one single most important asset that can help you save tons of money in your lifetime. If you have an excellent credit score, it works as your asset, and help you get lower interest rates. But, if your score is less, it may become your liability as lenders may hesitate to offer you a loan or offer you higher interest rates.

You can, however, easily, and quickly boost your credit score using the above points (even if you have zero credit history).

But you must always remember that your score evolves frequently. This makes it difficult to measure the impact of the single factor on the score. So, it is especially important that you should not stop or get complacent once you have boosted your credit score. Rather, you should regularly monitor your score to ensure it stays for you in the long-term. Also, you should make it a habit to evaluate how your score would get impacted when making any financial transactions.

References:

https://groww.in/blog/10-ways-to-help-you-improve-your-cibil-score/

https://clark.com/personal-finance-credit/how-to-improve-credit-score-quickly/

https://thelendersnetwork.com/how-to-improve-credit-score-fast/

https://studentloanhero.com/featured/how-to-improve-your-credit-score-in-30-days/

https://www.experian.com/blogs/ask-experian/credit-education/improving-credit/building-credit/

https://creditcards.usnews.com/articles/no-credit-score-what-happens-without-a-credit-history

https://www.incharge.org/debt-relief/credit-counseling/bad-credit/how-to-establish-credit-when-you-have-no-credit-history/

https://www.nerdwallet.com/article/finance/no-credit-score-zero-credit-score

https://www.experian.com/blogs/ask-experian/credit-education/improving-credit/improve-credit-score/

https://www.investopedia.com/how-to-improve-your-credit-score-4590097

https://www.debt.org/credit/improving-your-score/

https://www.credit.com/credit-scores/improve-credit-score-without-debt/

https://www.npr.org/2020/11/09/933053299/tricks-to-improve-your-credit-score

https://www.myknowledgebroker.com/blog/personal-insurance/how-to-raise-your-credit-score-by-100-points-in-45-days/

https://www.incharge.org/debt-relief/credit-counseling/credit-score-and-credit-report/

https://www.investopedia.com/terms/c/credit_score.asp

Congrats! Note from the Author/Publisher:

You've reached the end of the book!

Thank you for finishing **How to Boost Your Credit Score**

Looks like you enjoyed it!

If so, would you mind taking 30 seconds to leave a quick review on Amazon?

We worked hard to bring you books that you enjoy!

Plus, it helps authors like us produce more books like this in the future!

Follow link below:-
https://www.amazon.com/dp/B08PHW5TLD

Here's where to go to leave a review